Introduction

Have you always wanted to learn to knit?

Or perhaps you knitted years ago, but are unsure how to get started again.

If so, this book is for you. With our easy, step-by-step picture method you can learn all the basics of knitting in just a few hours — the technique for casting on, and two stitches: the knit stitch, and the purl stitch. That's all there is to it! Everything else is just a variation of these two stitches.

And you can do it all by yourself, with no one to help you. Our lessons are easy to follow, and we're right there beside you giving you special hints and helps along the way.

Once you feel comfortable with the basic techniques, you're ready to start one of our easy projects: an afghan, a baby set, a sweater, or a scarf and hat set. We've written all these patterns especially for the beginner.

We know you'll have fun learning with this book...and that you'll have years of enjoyment from your new skill.

Jean Leinhauser

Jean Leinhauser

Note to Left Handers:

Knitting is a two-handed process in which both hands are used almost equally. Therefore left handers do not need to worry about learning a different method. It may seem awkward at first, but this is true for all beginning knitters.

Getting Started

To knit, you need only a pair of knitting needles, some yarn, a tapestry needle and a pair of scissors. Later on, you can add all kinds of accessories, from needle point protectors to stitch holders to cable needles. But for now, your yarn and needles are all you really need.

Yarn

Yarn comes in a wonderful selection of materials, textures, sizes and colors, ranging from wool to metallic, lumpy to smooth, gossamer fine to chunky, and from the palest pastels to vibrant neon shades.

The most commonly used yarn, and the one you'll need for the lessons in this book, is worsted weight (sometimes called 4-ply). It is readily available in a wide variety of beautiful colors. Choose a light color for practice — it will be much easier to see the individual stitches.

Always read yarn labels carefully. The label will tell you how much yarn is in the skein or ball, in ounces, grams or yards; the type of yarn, how to care for it, and sometimes how to pull the yarn from the skein (and yes, there is a trick to this!). The label usually bears a dye lot number, which assures you that the color of each skein with this same number is identical. The same color may vary from dye lot to dye lot, creating unsightly variations in color when a project is finished. So when purchasing yarn for a project, be sure to match the dye lot number on the skeins.

You'll need a blunt-pointed sewing needle with an eye big enough to carry the yarn for weaving in ends and joining pieces. This is a size 16 steel tapestry needle. You can buy big plastic sewing needles called yarn needles, but they are not as good as the steel.

Knitting Needles

Knitting needles come in pairs of straight needles with a shaped point at one end and a knob at the other end of each needle so that the stitches won't slide off; in sets of four double-pointed needles used for making seamless small projects; and in circular form with a point at each end.

You will most often use straight needles, which are readily available in both aluminum and bamboo. Both materials are equally good. The straight needles come in two lengths: 10 inches and 14 inches. For our lessons, we will use the 10-inch length.

The needles also come in a variety of sizes, which refer to the diameter and thus the size of the stitch you can make with them. These are numbered from 0 (the smallest usually available) to 13 (the largest usually available). There are larger needles, but they are seldom used. For our lessons, we use a size 8 needle, an average size for use with worsted weight yarn.

Let's look at a knitting needle:

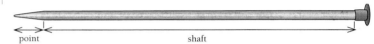

point   shaft

Now with your yarn and needles ready, let's get started. The pointed end of the needle is used to manipulate the yarn to make stitches. The long straight part of the needle, called the shaft, is where the stitches are carried once they are made. When the desired number of stitches has been worked onto the right needle, the left needle will be empty. Turn the right needle and place it in your left hand. The empty needle, now on the right, will carry the next row of stitches.

Hint: *It's very important to form the stitches well up onto the straight shaft, not on the point.*

Lesson 1

Casting On

Knitting always starts with a row of foundation stitches worked onto one needle. Making a foundation row is called casting on. Although there are several ways of casting on, the one which follows is easiest for beginners.

Step 1:

Make a slip knot on one needle as follows: Make a yarn loop, leaving about 4" length of yarn at free end.

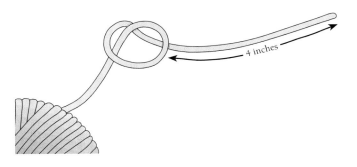

Insert knitting needle into loop and draw up yarn from free end to make a loop on needle.

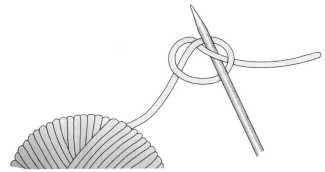

Pull yarn firmly, but not tightly, to form a slip knot on the shaft, not the point, of the needle.

Pull yarn end to tighten the loop. This slip knot counts as your first stitch.

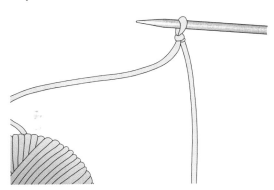

Step 2:

Place the needle with the knot in your left hand, placing the thumb and index finger close to the point of the needle, which helps you control it.

Step 3:

Hold the other needle with your right hand, again with your fingers close to the point. Grasp the needle firmly, but not tightly.

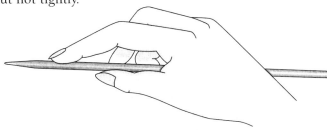

Step 4:

Your right hand will control the yarn coming from the ball; to help keep your tension even, hold the yarn loosely against the palm of your hand with three fingers, and then up and over your index finger. **A** and **B** show how this looks from above the hand and beneath the hand.

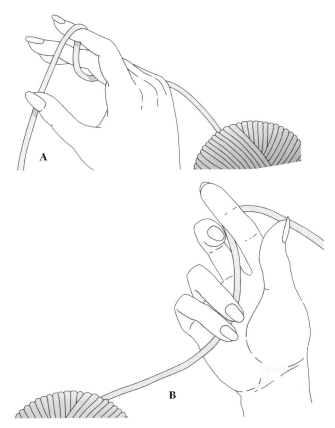

Step 5:
Insert the point of the right needle – from front to back – into the slip knot and under the left needle.

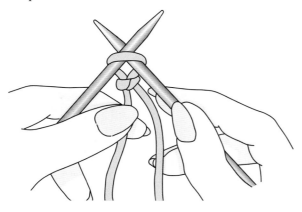

Step 6:
Continuing to hold left needle in your left hand, move left fingers over to brace right needle.

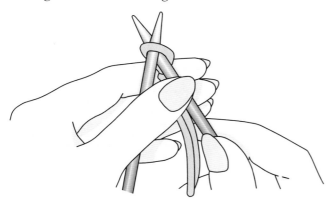

With right index finger, pick up the yarn from the ball

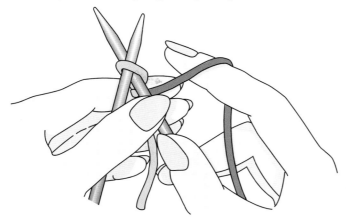

and, releasing right hand's grip on the right needle, bring yarn under and over the point of right needle.

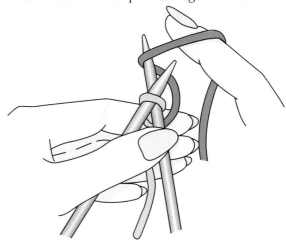

Step 7:
Returning right fingers to right needle, draw yarn through stitch with point of right needle.

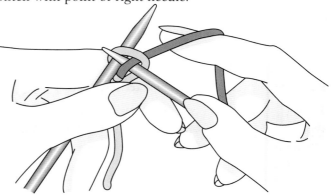

Step 8:
Slide left needle point into new stitch, then remove right needle.

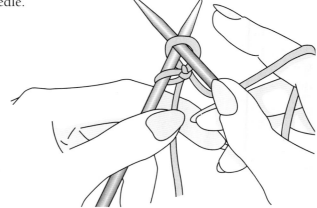

Step 9:

Pull ball yarn gently, but **not** tightly, to make stitch snug on needle; you should be able to slip the stitch back and forth on the shaft of the needle easily.

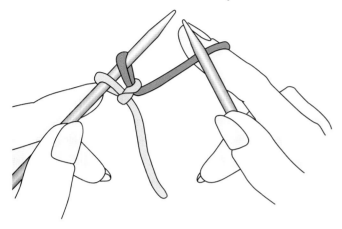

Hint:
Beginners usually knit very tightly, making it hard to slide the stitches on the needle. Try to relax; it is better to work too loosely in the beginning, than too tightly. Take care not to make your stitches on the point of the needle; instead, slide the needle shaft well through each stitch as you work. Always be sure to insert needle under full thickness of yarn, to avoid splitting the yarn.

You have now made one stitch, and there are two stitches on left needle (remember the slip knot counts as a stitch).

Step 10:

Insert point of right needle — from front to back — into stitch you've just made and **under** left needle.

Repeat Steps 4 through 8 for next stitch. Continue repeating Steps 4 through 8 until you have 24 stitches on the left needle. Be sure to pull each stitch up, off the point and onto the shaft of the needle.

Now stop, relax, get a cup of coffee or a soda, and look at your work. It's probably loose and uneven, which is normal for a beginner. As you practice and begin to feel less clumsy, your work will automatically become more even.

Now after all that work, guess what you're going to do next — destroy it! To do this, pull the needle out from the stitches, then wind the used yarn back on the skein or ball. Begin again and cast on 24 stitches, trying this time to work more evenly, keeping each stitch snug but **not** tight.

Lesson 2

The Knit Stitch

All knitting is made up of only two basic stitches, the knit stitch and the purl stitch. These are combined in many ways to create different effects and textures. And guess what — now you're half way to being a knitter — for you've already learned the knit stitch as you practiced casting on! That's because the first three steps of the knit stitch are exactly like casting on.

Step 1:
Hold the needle with the 24 cast-on stitches from Lesson 1 in your left hand. Insert point of right needle in first stitch, from front to back, just as in casting on.

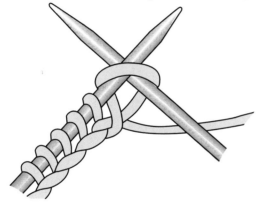

Step 2:
With right index finger, bring yarn from ball under and over point of right needle.

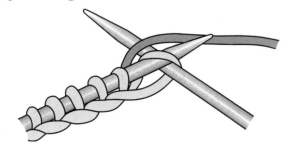

Step 3:
Draw yarn through stitch with right needle point.

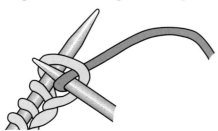

Step 4:
The next step now differs from casting on. Slip the loop on the left needle off, so the new stitch is entirely on the right needle.

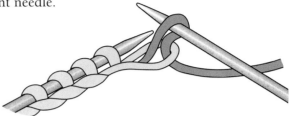

Now you've completed your first knit stitch! Repeat these four steps in each stitch remaining on the left needle. When all stitches are on the right needle and the left needle is free, another row has been completed. Turn right needle, hold it now in your left hand and take free needle in your right hand. Work another row of stitches in same manner as last row, taking care not to work tightly. Work 10 more rows of knit stitches.

The pattern formed by knitting every row is called **garter stitch** (we don't really know why!), and looks the same on both sides. When counting rows in garter stitch, each raised ridge (a ridge is indicated by the arrow in the photo below) indicates you have knitted two rows.

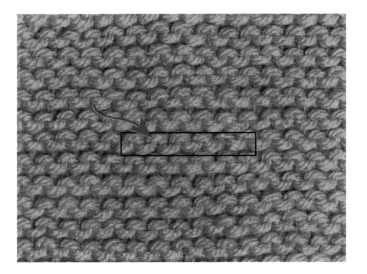

Break time!

The Purl Stitch

The reverse of the knit stitch is called the purl stitch. Instead of inserting the right needle point from front to back under the left needle (as you did for the knit stitch), you will now insert it from right to left, in front of the left needle. Work as follows on the 24 stitches already on your needle.

Step 1:

Insert right needle, from right to left, into first stitch, and in front of left needle.

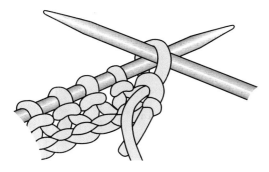

Step 2:

Holding yarn in front of work (side toward you), bring it around right needle counterclockwise.

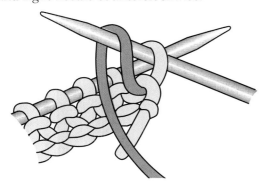

Step 3:

With right needle, pull yarn back through stitch.

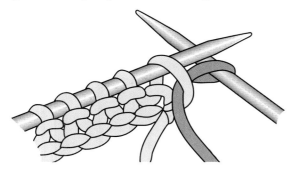

Slide stitch off left needle, leaving new stitch on right needle.

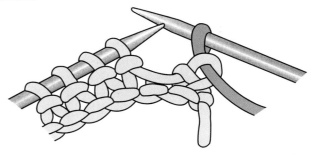

Your first purl stitch is now completed. Continue to repeat these three steps in every stitch across the row. The row you have just purled will be considered the wrong side of your work at the moment.

Now transfer the needle with stitches from right to left hand; the side of the work now facing you is called the right side of your work. Knit every stitch in the row; at end of row, transfer needle with stitches to left hand, then purl every stitch in the row. Knit across another row; purl across another row.

Now stop and look at your work; by alternating knit and purl rows, you are creating one of the most frequently used stitch patterns in knitting, **stockinette stitch**. Turn the work over to the right side; it should look like stitches in photo below.

The wrong side of the work should look like stitches in photo below.

Continue with your practice piece, alternately knitting and purling rows, until you feel comfortable with the needles and yarn. As you work you'll see that your piece will begin to look more even.

Lesson 4

Correcting Mistakes

Dropped Stitches

Each time you knit or purl a stitch, take care to pull the stitch completely off the left needle after finishing the new stitch. Otherwise, you will be adding stitches when you don't want to. But don't let a stitch slip off the needle **before** you've knitted or purled it — that's called a dropped stitch. Even expert knitters drop a stitch now and then, but a dropped stitch must be picked up and put back on the needle. If not, the stitch will "run" down the length of the piece just like a run in a stocking!

If you notice the dropped stitch right away, and it has not run down more than one row, you can usually easily place it back on the needle.

But if it has dropped several rows, you'll find it easier to use a crochet hook to work the stitch back up to the needle. Here's how.

On the knit side (right side of work) of the stockinette stitch, insert the crochet hook into the dropped stitch from front to back, under the horizontal strand in the row above.

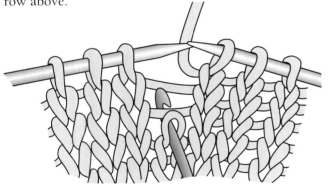

Hook the horizontal strand above and pull through the loop on the crochet hook. Continue in this manner until you reach the last row worked, then transfer the loop from the crochet hook to the left needle, being careful not to twist it.

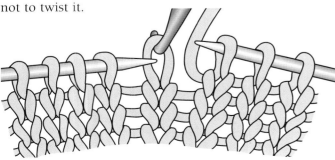

Unraveling Stitches

Sometimes it is necessary to unravel a large number of stitches, even down several rows, to correct a mistake. Whenever possible, carefully unravel the stitches one-by-one by putting the left needle into the row below and undoing the stitch above, until the mistake is reached.

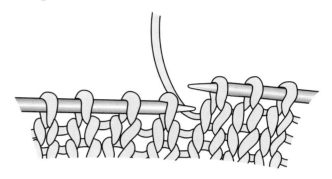

If several rows need to be unraveled, carefully slide all stitches off the needle and unravel each row down to the row in which the error occurred. Then unravel this row, stitch by stitch, placing each stitch back on the needle in the correct position, without twisting it.

Lesson 5

Binding Off

Now you've learned how to cast on, and to knit and purl the stitches; next you need to know how to take the stitches off the needle once you've finished a piece.

The process used to secure the stitches is called binding off. Let's bind off your practice piece. Be careful to work loosely for this procedure, and begin with the right side (the knit side) of your work facing you.

Knit Bind-Off
Step 1:
Knit the first 2 stitches. Now insert left needle into the first of the 2 stitches, the one you knitted first,

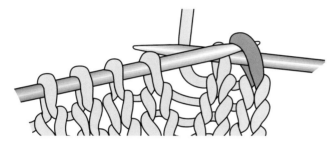

and pull it over the second stitch and completely off the needle. You have now bound off one stitch.

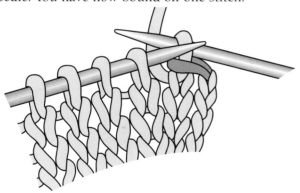

Step 2:
Knit one more stitch; insert left needle into first stitch on right needle and pull first stitch over the new stitch and completely off the needle. Another stitch is now bound off.

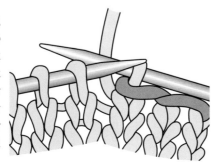

Repeat Step 2 four times more; now knit each of the 17 stitches remaining on the left needle. You have bound off 6 stitches on the knit side of your work.

To bind off on the purl side, turn your practice piece so the wrong side of your work is facing you.

Purl Bind-Off
Step 1:
Purl the first 2 stitches. Now insert left needle into the first stitch purled on right needle,

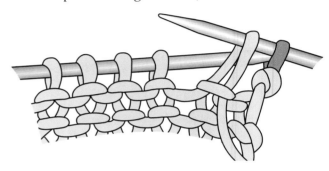

and pull it over the second stitch and completely off the needle. You have now bound off one stitch.

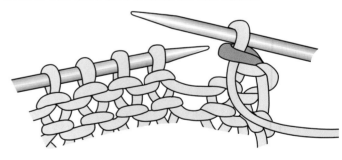

Step 2:
Purl one more stitch; insert left needle into first stitch on right needle and pull first stitch over the new stitch and completely off the needle. Another stitch is bound off.

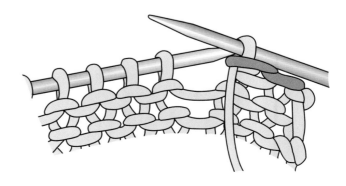

Repeat Step 2 four times more; now purl each of the 11 stitches remaining on the left needle.

Turn your work so that the right side is facing you; bind off 6 stitches in the same manner that you bound off the first 6 stitches on this side, then knit remaining stitches.

Turn your work and bind off the remaining stitches on the wrong side; there will be one stitch left on the needle and you are ready to "finish off" or "end off" the yarn. To do this, cut yarn leaving about a 4" end. With needle, draw this end up and then through the final stitch to secure it.

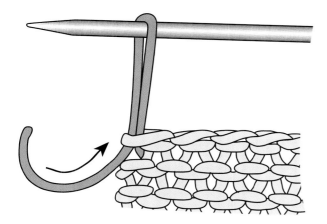

You have just learned to bind off knit stitches on the right side of your work and purl stitches on the wrong side of your work. When you wish to bind off in a pattern stitch, where some stitches in a row have been knitted and others purled, knit the knit stitches and purl the purl stitches as you work across the row.

Always bind off loosely to maintain the same amount of stretch or "give" at the edge as in the rest of your work. If bind off is too tight at the neckband ribbing of a pullover sweater, for example, the sweater will not fit over your head!

Hint:
You can insure the binding off being loose enough if you replace the needle in your right hand with a needle one size larger.

Lesson 6

Increasing

To shape knitted pieces, you will make them wider or narrower by increasing or decreasing a certain number of stitches from time to time.

Begin a new practice piece by casting on 12 stitches. Work 4 rows of garter stitch (remember this means you will **knit** every row); then on the next row, purl across (this purl side now becomes the wrong side of the work, since you will now begin working in stockinette stitch). Knit one more row, then purl one more row. You are now ready to practice increasing.

Although there are many ways to increase, this is used most often.

Knitting (or Purling) 2 stitches in One.
On your practice piece (with the right side facing you), work as follows in the first stitch:

Step 1:
Insert tip of right needle from front to back of stitch, and knit it in the usual manner but don't remove the stitch from the left needle.

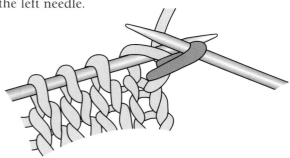

Step 2:
Insert right needle (from front to back) into **back** loop of same stitch, and knit it again, this time slipping the stitch off the left needle. You have now increased one stitch.

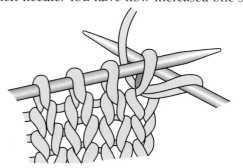

Knit across the row until one stitch remains, then increase again by repeating Steps 1 and 2. You should now have 14 stitches. Purl one row; knit one row.

On your next row, the purl side, again increase in the first stitch. To increase on the purl side, insert needle and purl in the usual manner, but don't remove the stitch from the left needle. Then insert needle (from back to front) into back loop of same stitch;

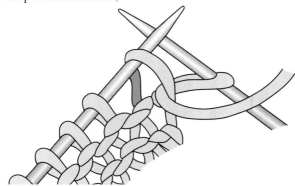

purl it again, this time slipping the stitch off. Then purl across to last stitch; increase again. You should now have 16 stitches.

Now knit one row and purl one row, without increasing.

Decreasing

Decreasing, Method 1

Knit (or Purl) 2 Stitches Together

In this method, you simply knit 2 stitches as one. Knit each of the first 2 stitches on your practice piece, then decrease as follows.

Step 1:

Insert needle in usual manner but through the fronts of both of the first 2 stitches on the left needle.

Step 2:

Bring yarn under and over point of needle;

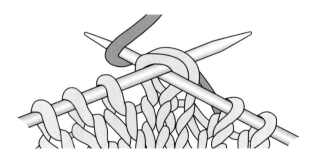

draw yarn through both stitches; slip stitches off left needle and one new stitch will be on the right needle.

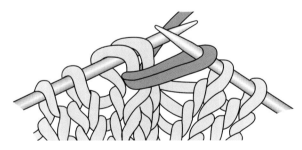

You have decreased one stitch. Knit across to the last 4 stitches; repeat Steps 1 and 2 again to decrease another stitch, then knit the last 2 stitches. You should now have 14 stitches.

This decrease can also be worked on the purl side. On the next row of your practice piece, purl 2 stitches, then insert needle in the fronts of next 2 stitches and purl them as if they were one stitch. Purl to the last 4 stitches, decrease again; purl remaining 2 stitches.

Decreasing, Method 2

Pass Slipped Stitch Over

This method is often used in the shaping of raglans or other pieces where a definite decrease line is desired. To use this method you must first know how to "slip" a stitch.

When instructions say to slip a stitch, this means you will slip it from the left needle to the right, without working it. To do this, insert right needle into stitch as if you were going to purl it (even if it's a knit stitch); but instead of purling, slip the stitch from left needle to right needle.

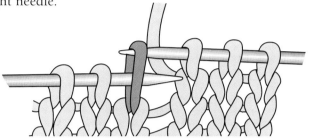

> **Hint:**
> *Always insert needle as to purl when slipping a stitch, unless instructions specify "slip as to knit"; in that case, insert needle in position for knitting, and slip the stitch in same manner.*

Now that you know how to slip a stitch, you can practice the second method of decreasing. On your practice piece, knit the first 3 stitches. Instructions to decrease may read: "Slip 1, knit 1, pass slipped stitch over". To do this, work as follows:

Step 1:

Slip the next stitch, as to purl.

Step 2:

Knit the next stitch.

Step 3:

Pass the slipped stitch over the knitted stitch by using point of left needle to lift slipped stitch over the next stitch and completely off the needle.

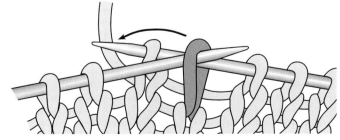

You may wish to continue practicing Steps 1, 2 and 3 across the row. This decrease can also be worked on the purl side. To do so, purl a few stitches. Slip next stitch, purl the next stitch, pass slipped stitch over purled stitch. Purl remaining stitches, then bind off all stitches.

Lesson 8

Ribbing

Sometimes you want a piece of knitting to fit more closely — such as at the neck, wrists or bottom of a sweater. To do this, a combination of knit and purl stitches alternating in the same row, called ribbing, creates an elastic effect. To practice ribbing, start a new piece by casting on 24 stitches loosely (always cast on for ribbing loosely, or the first row won't stretch enough).

Knit 2, Purl 2 Ribbing

Pattern Row: Knit 2 stitches, then bring yarn to **front of work** and purl 2 stitches; bring yarn to **back of work** and knit 2 stitches; **yarn to front** again, purl 2 stitches.

> **Note:**
> *You may tend to add stitches accidentally by forgetting to move the yarn to the front before purling, or to the back before knitting. Remembering to move the yarn, repeat this knit 2, purl 2 alternating pattern across the row.*

Work this same Pattern Row eleven times more (12 rows of ribbing in all). Your work should look like this. Practice this ribbing until you feel comfortable with it.

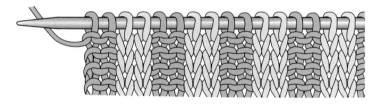

> **Hint:**
> *If you have trouble distinguishing a knit stitch or a purl stitch, remember that the smooth stitches are knit stitches and the bumpy ones are purl stitches.*

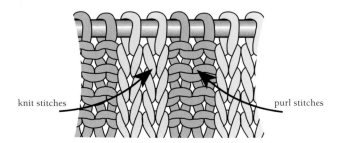

knit stitches   purl stitches

Now knit one row, then purl one row, and then bind off loosely, remembering to knit the knit stitches and purl the purl stitches. Look at the work and see how the ribbing draws it in.

Knit 1, Purl 1 Ribbing

This rib stitch pattern produces a finer ribbing, and is often used on baby clothes or on garments knitted with light weight yarns.

Again cast on 24 stitches.

Pattern Row: Knit the first stitch, yarn to front, purl the next stitch; yarn to back, knit next stitch; yarn to front, purl next stitch. Continue across row, alternating one knit stitch with one purl stitch.

Work this same Pattern Row 11 times more (12 rows of ribbing). Your work should look like this.

Practice this ribbing for several more rows, again knit one row and purl one row, then bind off.

Lesson 9

Joining Yarn

New yarn should be added only at the **beginning** of a row, never in the middle of a row, unless this is required for a color pattern change. To add yarn, tie the new strand around the old strand, making a knot at the edge of work, leaving at least a 4" end on both old and new strands. Then proceed to work with the new yarn. The ends will be hidden later by weaving in.

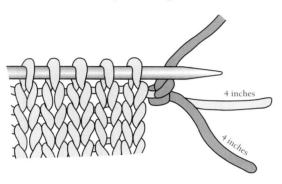

Lesson 10

Gauge and Measuring

This is the most important lesson of all, for if you don't work to gauge, your knitted garments will never fit correctly.

Gauge simply means the number of stitches per inch, and the number of rows per inch, that result from a specified yarn worked with needles in a specified size. But since everyone knits differently — some loosely, some tightly, some in between — the measurements of individual work will vary greatly, even when the knitters use the exact same pattern and the exact same size yarn and needles. The photo shows the variance clearly. The two pieces were knitted by two different people — but each used the same pattern, the same yarn, and the same needle size.

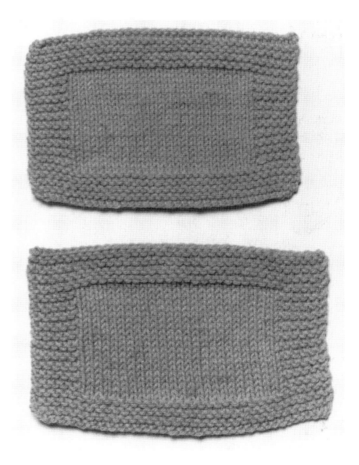

Needle sizes given in instructions are merely guides, and should never be used without making a 4" square sample swatch to check your gauge. *It is your responsibility to make sure you achieve the gauge specified in the pattern.* To achieve this gauge, you may need to use a different needle size — either larger or smaller — than that specified in the pattern. Always change to larger or smaller needles if necessary to achieve gauge.

Here's how to check your gauge. At the beginning of every knit pattern you'll find a gauge given, like this (note the use of abbreviations):

Gauge:
In stock st, with size 7 needles, 5 sts = 1"
6 rows = 1"

This means that you will work your gauge swatch in stockinette stitch, and will try to achieve a gauge of 5 stitches and 6 rows to 1". You must make a gauge swatch at least 4" square to adequately test your work. So, cast on 20 stitches (5 stitches measure 1"; for a 4" width, multiply 5 times 4 to get 20 stitches). Work in stockinette stitch for 24 rows (6 rows measure 1"; for a 4" length, multiply 6 by 4 to get 24 rows). Loosely bind off all stitches.

Place the swatch on a flat surface and pin it out, being careful not to stretch it. Measure the outside edges; the swatch should be 4" square.

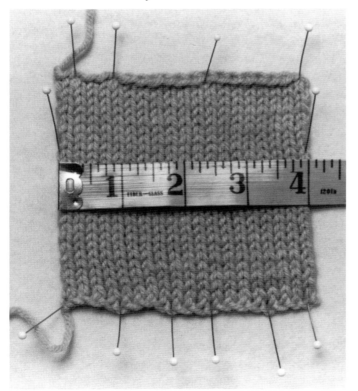

Now measure the center 2", and count the actual stitches and rows per inch.

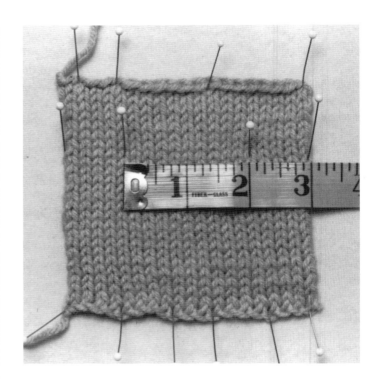

If you have **more** stitches or rows per inch than specified, make another swatch with a size **larger** needles.

If you have **fewer** stitches or rows per inch than specified, make another swatch with a size **smaller** needles.

Making gauge swatches before beginning a project takes time and is a bother. But if you don't make the effort to do this important step, you'll never be able to create attractive, well-fitting projects.

Once you've begun a project, it's a good idea to keep checking your gauge every few inches; if you become relaxed, you'll find yourself knitting more loosely; if you tense up, your knitting will become tighter. To keep your gauge, you may need to change needle sizes in the middle of a project.

Hint:
Sometimes you'll find that you have the correct stitch gauge, but can't get the row gauge even with a change in needle size. If so, the stitch gauge is more important than the row gauge, with one exception; raglan sweaters. In knitting raglans, the armhole depth is based on row gauge, so you must achieve both stitch and row gauge.

Lesson 11

Reading Patterns
(abbreviations, symbols and terms)

Knitting patterns are written in a special language, full of abbreviations, asterisks, parentheses, and other symbols and terms. These short forms are used so instructions will not take up too much space. They may seem confusing at first, but once understood, it is easy to follow them.

Abbreviations

beg	begin(ning)
dec	decrease(-ing)
Fig	figure
inc.	increase(-ing)
K	knit
lp(s)	loop(s)
P	purl
patt	pattern
prev	previous
PSSO	pass slipped stitch over
rem	remain(ing)
rep	repeat(ing)
sk	skip
sl	slip
sl st(s)	slip stitch(es)
sp(s)	space(s)
st(s)	stitch(es)
stock st	stockinette stitch
tog	together
YO	yarn over

Symbols

* An asterisk is used to mark the beginning of a portion of instructions which will be worked more than once; thus, "rep from * twice" means after working the instructions once, repeat the instructions following the asterisk twice more (3 times in all).

: The number after a colon at the end of a row indicates the number of stitches you should have when the row/round has been completed.

( ) Parentheses are used to enclose instructions which should be worked the exact number of times specified immediately following the parentheses, such as (K1, P1) twice.

They are also used to list the garment sizes and to provide additional information to clarify instructions.

Terms

WORK IN PATT AS ESTABLISHED is usually used in a pattern stitch, and this means to continue following the pattern stitch as it is set up (established) on the needle, working any subsequent increases or decreases in such a way that the established pattern remains the same (usually, working them at the beginning or end of a row), outside the established pattern area.

WORK EVEN means to continue to work in the pattern as established, without working any increases or decreases.

Lesson 12

Finishing

Many a well-knitted garment, worked exactly to gauge, ends up looking sloppy and amateurish, simply because of bad finishing. To finish a knitted garment requires no special skill, but it does require time, attention, and a knowledge of basic techniques.

Picking up Stitches

You will often need to pick up a certain number of stitches along an edge, such as around a sweater neckline or armhole, so that ribbing or an edging can be worked. The pattern instructions will usually state clearly where and how many stitches to pick up. Although this is not difficult, it is often done incorrectly and the results look messy. Picking up is best done with a crochet hook, with the stitches then slipped from it to a knitting needle.

To pick up a stitch, hold the knitting with its right side facing you. Hold yarn from skein in your left hand, behind the work, and hold crochet hook in your right hand. Insert hook into work from front to back, one stitch (at least 2 threads) from the edge;

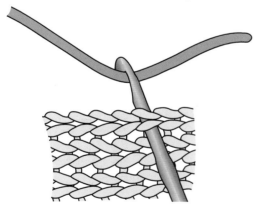

hook yarn and pull a loop back through work, making one stitch on hook.

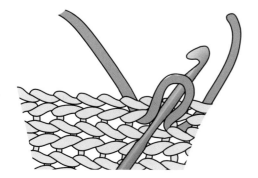

Now slip stitch off crochet hook and onto knitting needle of the correct size for ribbing, being sure to have the stitch in the correct position, without twisting it.

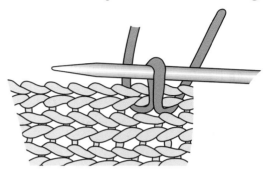

To space your stitches evenly when picking up, pick up one stitch for each stitch when working across stitches in a horizontal row, and pick up about 3 stitches for every 4 rows when working along ends of rows. If a large number of stitches is to be picked up, it is best to mark off the edge into equal sections, then pick up the same number of stitches in each section.

Weaving in Ends

Before blocking and sewing the seams, weave in all the yarn ends securely. To do this, use a size 16 tapestry needle and weave the yarn end through the backs of stitches, first weaving about 2" in one direction and then 1" in the reverse direction. Cut off excess yarn. (**Note:** *Never weave in more than one yarn end at a time.*)

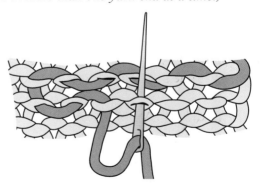

Blocking

Blocking simply means "setting" each piece into its final size and shape. (**Note:** *Be sure to check the yarn label before blocking, as some synthetic yarns and mohair yarns are ruined if they are blocked.*)

To block, moisten each piece first, either by washing or dampening with a light water spray. Then place each piece out on a padded flat surface (terry toweling provides adequate padding) right side up and away from direct sunlight. Smooth out each piece to correct size and shape, using your fingers and the palms of your hands, being sure to keep the stitches and rows in straight alignment. Use rust-proof straight pins to hold the edges in place. Let pieces dry completely before removing.

If further blocking is required, use steam from a steam iron. Hold the iron close to the knitted piece and allow the steam to penetrate the fabric. Never rest the iron directly on the piece — knitting should never have a pressed flat look. Let dry completely before removing.

> **Important Note:**
> *Never press ribbing, garter stitch, cables, or textured patterns as in Irish knits.*

Sewing Seams

Your pattern will usually tell you in what order to assemble the pieces. Use the same yarn as used in the garment to sew the seams, unless the yarn is too thick, in which case use a thinner yarn in a matching color. Pin seams before sewing, carefully matching stitches and rows as much as possible.

Invisible Seam: This seam gives a smooth and neat appearance, as it weaves the edges together invisibly from the right side. To join vertical edges, such as side seams or underarm sleeve seams, sew the edges together as shown working one stitch in from each edge.

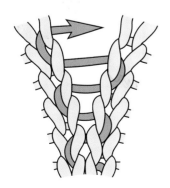

To join horizontal edges, such as shoulder seams, weave the edges together as shown drawing yarn up as you work.

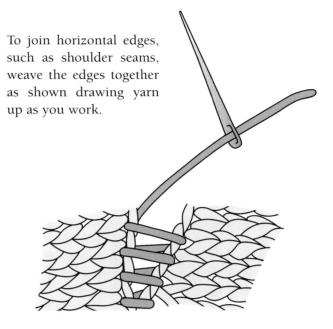

Backstitch Seam: This method gives a strong, firm joining, and is usually used when the seam will have a lot of stress or pull on it. To join, hold both pieces with right sides together, then sew through both thicknesses as shown below.

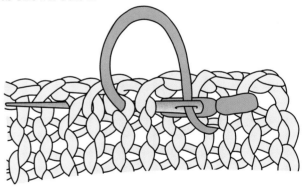

> **Hint:**
> *When seaming, do not draw the stitches too tightly, as the joining should have the same stretch or give as in the knitted garment.*

You've graduated!

Now you've learned the basics of knitting. Was it fun? You can now go on to make your first project.

Hat and Scarf

These are worked entirely in K2, P2 ribbing. But because it is difficult to measure gauge on ribbing, the gauge is given in stock st. So you will make a stock st swatch to check your gauge. We've shown the set in off white, but you can of course make it any color you like.

Size:
One size fits most adults

Materials:
Worsted weight yarn, 14 oz (980 yds) off white, or color of your choice

Size 9, 14" straight knitting needles, or size required for gauge

Size 16 tapestry needle

Gauge:
9 sts = 2" in stock st

Instructions

Hat
Cast on 108 sts loosely.

Row 1: K1, P2, * K2, P2; rep from * across row, ending K1.

Row 2: P1, K2, * P2, K2; rep from * across row, ending K1.

Rep Rows 1 and 2 until Hat measures 11" from cast-on edge.

Crown:
Row 1: K1, P2 tog; * K2 tog; P2 tog; rep from * across row, ending K1: 55 sts.

Row 2: P1, * K2 tog; rep from * across row: 28 sts.

Row 3: * K2 tog; rep from * across row: 14 sts.

Row 4: * K2 tog; rep from * across row.

Cut yarn leaving an 18" end for sewing.

Thread end into yarn needle; thread through sts on needle twice, removing needle as you thread. Pull yarn end tight. With right side facing you, weave seam from crown to cast-on edge.

Weave in all loose ends.

Turn cast-on edge up to form cuff.

Scarf
Cast on 52 sts loosely.

Row 1: P1, K2, * P2, K2; rep from * across row, ending P1. 𝄃𝄃

Row 2: K1, P2, * K2, P2; rep from * across row, ending K1. 𝄌

Rep Rows 1 and 2 until scarf measures 72" long.

Bind off loosely in pattern (knit the knit sts and purl the purl sts).

Weave in all loose ends.

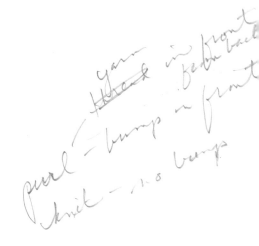

Baby Bonnet and Sweater

This charming set makes a perfect gift to welcome the new baby. We've made it in a sweet print yarn, but you can also make it in any solid color.

The bonnet and sweater are worked both on straight needles and, to allow for shaping, on circular needles. To use these, see Using Circular Needles *in the afghan pattern instructions on page 31.*

In this pattern, YOs are used to create a decorative trim. Be sure you check your stitch gauge carefully, changing to a different needle size if necessary to achieve gauge. This design is worked rather tightly, and if you are a loose knitter the size will be wrong.

Size:
6 months

Materials:
Worsted weight yarn, 8 1/2 oz (595 yds) variegated, or solid color of your choice
Size 5, 14" straight knitting needles, or size required for gauge
Size 5, 24" circular knitting needles
Size G aluminum crochet hook
One large stitch holder
Two med stitch holders
Size 16 tapestry needle
2 yds 1/4"-wide white satin ribbon
Sewing needle and matching thread

Gauge:
11 sts = 2" in stock st

Instructions
Bonnet
With straight needles, cast on 32 sts.

Row 1 (right side): Knit.

Row 2: Purl.

Row 3: K1, * K2 tog; YO; rep from * 13 times more; K2 tog, K1: 31 sts.

Row 4: Purl.

Row 5: Knit.

Row 6: Purl.

Row 7: K1, sl 1, K1, PSSO; K6; * YO, K1, YO, K2; rep from * 4 times more; K5, K2 tog: 39 sts.

Rows 8 through 10: Rep Rows 4 through 6.

Row 11: K1, sl 1, K1, PSSO; K6; * YO, K1, YO, K4; rep from * 4 times more; K3, K2 tog: 47 sts.

Rows 12 through 14: Rep Rows 4 through 6.

Row 15: K1, sl 1, K1, PSSO; K6; * YO, K1, YO, K6; rep from * 4 times more; K1, K2 tog: 55 sts.

Rows 16 through 18: Rep Rows 4 through 6.

Row 19: K1, sl 1, K1, PSSO; K6; * YO, K1, YO, K8; rep from * 3 times more; YO, K1, YO, K7, K2 tog: 63 sts.

Rows 20 through 22: Rep Rows 4 through 6.

Row 23: K1, sl 1, K1, PSSO; K6; * YO, K1, YO, K10; rep from * 3 times more; YO, K1, YO, K7, K2 tog: 71 sts.

Rows 24 through 26: Rep Rows 4 through 6.

Rows 27 through 40: Rep Rows 1 and 2 seven times.

Row 41: Bind off next 24 sts; knit across: 47 sts.

Row 42: Bind off next 24 sts; purl across: 23 sts.

Crown:
Rows 43 through 52: Rep Rows 1 and 2 five times.

Row 53: Sl 1, K1, PSSO; * K5, K2 tog; rep from * twice more: 19 sts.

Row 54: Purl.

Rows 55 through 58: Rep Rows 1 and 2 twice.

Row 59: Sl 1, K1, PSSO; * K4, K2 tog; rep from * once more; K3, K2 tog: 15 sts.

Row 60: Purl.

Rows 61 through 66: Rep Rows 1 and 2 three times.

Bind off.

Hold edge of top section and bound off row of sides with right sides tog. Sew seams to form crown.

Crown Edging:
Beg and ending at side of Row 3, with circular needle and crochet hook, pick up 32 sts evenly spaced along side, 14 sts across crown, and 32 sts along other side: 78 sts.

Row 1: Knit.

Row 2: Purl.

Row 3: K2, * YO, K2 tog; rep from * to last 2 sts; YO, K2.

Row 4: Purl.

Row 5: Knit.

Bind off as to purl.

Weave in all loose ends.

Finishing
Step 1: Fold crown edge under at Row 3 forming peaks; sew in place.

Step 2: Cut ribbon into 4 equal lengths. Tie one end of each length into bow; sew one length to each side of Bonnet at lower crown edge. Set aside remaining ribbon.

Sweater
Starting at neckline with circular needles, cast on 58 sts.

Row 1 (right side): Knit.

Row 2 and all even numbered rows: Purl.

Row 3: K1, YO, * K2 tog; YO; rep from * 27 times more; K1: 59 sts.

Row 5: Knit.

Row 7: K3, * YO, K2 tog; YO, K3; rep from * 10 times more; K1: 70 sts.

Row 9: Knit.

Row 11: K4, * YO, K1, YO, K5; rep from * 10 times more: 92 sts.

Row 13: Knit.

Row 15: K5, * YO, K1, YO, K7; rep from * 9 times more; YO, K1, YO, K6: 114 sts.

Row 17: Knit.

Row 19: K6, * YO, K1, YO, K9; rep from * 9 times more; YO, K1, YO, K7: 136 sts.

Row 21: Knit.

Row 23: K7, * YO, K1, YO, K11; rep from * 9 times more; YO, K1, YO, K8: 158 sts.

Row 25: Knit.

Row 27: K8, * YO, K1, YO, K13; rep from * 9 times more; YO, K1, YO, K9: 180 sts.

Row 29: Knit.

Row 31: K9, * YO, K1, YO, K15; rep from * 9 times more; YO, K1, YO, K10: 202 sts.

Row 33: Knit.

Row 35: K10, * YO, K1, YO, K17; rep from * 9 times more; YO, K1, YO, K11: 224 sts.

Row 37 (dividing row): For left front, K38, sl these sts onto med stitch holder; for left sleeve, K37; for back, K74, sl these sts onto large holder; for right sleeve, K37; for right front, sl rem 38 sts onto med holder.

Sleeves:
Note: Both sleeves are worked at the same time with separate balls of yarn. Let yarn not in use hang on wrong side of work until needed. Purl across right sleeve; join another ball of yarn in first st of left sleeve, purl across left sleeve.

Row 1: Knit (across both sleeves).

Row 2: Purl (across both sleeves).

Rows 3 and 4: Rep Rows 1 and 2.

Row 5: Sl 1, K1, PSSO; knit to last 2 sts of left sleeve; K2 tog; on right sleeve, sl 1, K1, PSSO; knit to last 2 sts, K2 tog.

Row 6: Purl.

Rep Rows 1 through 6 four times more. At end of last rep, 27 sts.

Edging:
Row 1: K1, * YO, K2 tog; rep from * 12 times more.

Row 2: Purl.

Row 3: Knit.

Row 4: Purl.

Bind off both sleeves.

Body:
Slip stitches on holder to circular needle. With right side facing you, join yarn in first st of right front.

Row 1: Knit across right front.

Row 2: Purl across right front, slip stitches from large holder onto left-hand needle; purl across back; slip stitches from med stitch holder onto left-hand needle; purl across left front: 150 sts.

Row 3: Knit.

Row 4: Purl.

Rows 5 through 36: Rep Rows 3 and 4 sixteen times.

Lower Edging:
Row 1: K2, * YO, K2 tog; rep from * across row to last 2 sts; YO, K2.

Row 2: Purl.

Row 3: Knit.

Row 4: Purl.

Bind off.

Center Front Edging:
With straight needles and crochet hook, and beg and ending at YO rows of body, pick up 50 sts evenly spaced along one center front edge.

Row 1: Knit.

Row 2: Purl.

Row 3: K2, * YO, K2 tog; rep from * across row to last 2 sts; YO, K2.

Row 4: Purl.

Row 5: Knit.

Bind off as to purl.

Rep for other center front edging.

Weave in all loose ends.

Finishing
Step 1: Sew sleeve seams.

Step 2: Turn neckline to wrong side at first YO row, and sew in place.

Step 3: Turn edge of body to wrong side at first YO row, and sew in place.

Step 4: Turn edge of each sleeve to wrong side at first YO row, and sew in place.

Step 5: Turn edge of each center front edge to wrong side at first YO row, and sew in place.

Step 6: Tack one ribbon length with bow to each side of center front neckline.

Boat Neck Sweater

This is an easy to wear, comfortable sweater that's good for a first project. It is worked in four pieces: a back, a front and two sleeves, which are then sewn together. You may want to make several in different colors.

Sizes:
Chest: 34" 36" 38" 40"
Finished chest: 38" 40" 42" 44"
Note: *Instructions are written for small size. Changes for larger sizes are in parentheses.*

Materials:
Worsted weight yarn, 18 (19, 20, 21) oz [1260 (1330, 1400, 1470) yds] off white, or color of your choice
Size 7, 14" straight knitting needles, or size required for gauge
Size 5, 14" straight knitting needles

Gauge:
5 sts = 1" in stock st
6 rows = 1" in stock st

Instructions

Back
With larger size needles, cast on 97 (101, 107, 111) sts. Change to smaller size needles.

Ribbing:
Row 1 (right side): K1, * P1, K1; rep from * across row.

Row 2: P1, * K1, P1; rep from * across row.

Rows 3 through 14: Rep Rows 1 and 2 six times. At end of Row 14, change to larger size needles.

Body:
Row 1: Knit.

Row 2: Purl.

Rep Rows 1 and 2 until piece measures 15" (15", 16", 16") from cast-on edge.

Note: *Mark each end of last row worked with thread for beg of armhole.*

Rep Rows 1 and 2 until piece measures 20" (20", 22", 22") from cast-on edge.

Neckline Ribbing:
Rows 1 through 14: Continuing with larger size needles, rep Rows 1 and 2 of ribbing seven times.

Bind off loosely in ribbing (knit the knit sts, and purl the purl sts).

Front
Work same as for Back.

Sleeves (make 2)
With larger size needles, cast on 57 (59, 61, 63) sts. Change to smaller size needles.

Ribbing:
Row 1 (right side): K1, * P1, K1; rep from * across row.

Row 2: P1, * K1, P1; rep from * across row.

Rows 3 through 14: Rep Rows 1 and 2 six times. At end of Row 14, change to larger size needles.

Arm:
Row 1: Knit.

Row 2: Purl.

Rows 3 through 6: Rep Rows 1 and 2 twice.

Row 7: Inc (knit in front and back); knit to last st, inc.

Rep Rows 2 through 7, 13 (13, 14, 14) times more, or until sleeve measures about 17" (17", 18", 18") from cast-on edge.

Next Row: Purl.

Bind off.

Finishing
Step 1: Hold Front and Back with right sides together. Sew shoulder seams, leaving about 10" opening in center for neck.

Step 2: Sew sleeves to body between markers, matching center of sleeves to shoulder seams.

Weave in all loose ends.

Striped Sweater

This is the same basic sweater as the solid-color Boat Neck Sweater *on page 26, but in this version we've jazzed it up with stripes. You can do the stripes in whatever colors you like.*

Sizes:
Chest: 34" 36" 38" 40"
Finished chest: 38" 40" 42" 44"
Note: *Instructions are written for small size. Changes for larger sizes are in parentheses.*

Materials:
Worsted weight yarn, 16 (16 1/2, 17, 17 1/2) oz [1120 (1155, 1190, 1225) yds] off white; 3 1/2 oz (245 yds) each, beige and dk brown
Size 7, 14" straight knitting needles, or size required for gauge
Size 5, 14" straight knitting needles

Gauge:
5 sts = 1" in stock st
6 rows = 1" in stock st

Instructions

Back
With larger size needles and off white, cast on 97 (101, 107, 111) sts. Change to smaller size needles.

Ribbing:
Row 1 (right side)**:** K1, * P1, K1; rep from * across row.

Row 2: P1, * K1, P1; rep from * across row.

Rows 3 through 14: Rep Rows 1 and 2 six times. At end of Row 14, change to larger size needles.

Body:
Row 1: Knit.

Row 2: Purl.

Rows 3 through 10: Rep Rows 1 and 2 four times. At end of Row 10, finish off, off white; join dk brown.

Row 11: Knit. Finish off dk brown; join off white.

Row 12: Purl.

Rows 13 through 20: Rep Rows 1 and 2 four times.

Row 21: Knit. Finish off, off white; join dk brown.

Row 22: Purl. Finish off dk brown; join beige.

Rows 23 through 28 (28, 30, 30): Rep Rows 1 and 2 three (three, four, four) times. At end of last row, finish off beige; join off white.

Rows 29 (29, 31, 31) and 30 (30, 32, 32): Rep Rows 1 and 2. At end of last row, finish off, off white; join beige.

Rows 31 (31, 33, 33) through 36 (36, 40, 40): Rep Rows 1 and 2 three (three, four, four) times. At end of last row, finish off beige; join dk brown.

Mark each end of last row worked with thread for armhole.

Note: *Piece should measure about 15" (15", 16", 16") from cast-on edge.*

Row 37 (37, 41, 41): Knit. Finish off dk brown; join off white.

Rep Rows 2 through 37 (37, 41, 41) once more.

Rep Rows 2 through 21 once. At end of last row, do not finish off, off white; do not join dk brown.

Next Row: Purl.

Neckline Ribbing:
Rows 1 through 14: Continuing with off white and larger size needles, rep Rows 1 and 2 of ribbing seven times.

Bind off loosely in ribbing (knit the knit sts, and purl the purl sts).

Front
Work same as for Back.

Sleeves (make 2)
With off white and larger size needles, cast on 57 (59, 61, 63) sts. Change to smaller size needles.

Ribbing:
Rows 1 through 14: Rep Rows 1 through 14 of Back Ribbing.

Note: *Remember change to larger size needles.*

Arm:
Row 1: Knit.
Row 2: Purl.
Rows 3 through 6: Rep Rows 1 and 2 twice.

Row 7: Inc in first st, knit across row to last st; inc in last st.
Row 8: Purl.

Row 33: Knit. Finish off dk brown; join off white.
Row 34: Purl.
Rows 35 and 36: Rep Rows 1 and 2.

Row 37: Rep Row 7.
Row 38: Purl.
Rows 39 through 42: Rep Rows 1 and 2 twice.

Row 43: Rep Row 7. Finish off, off white; join dk brown.
Row 44: Purl. Finish off dk brown; join off white.
Rows 45 through 48: Rep Rows 1 and 2 twice.

Row 49: Rep Row 7.
Row 50: Purl.
Rows 51 and 52: Rep Rows 1 and 2.

Rows 53: Knit.
Row 54: Purl. Finish off, off white; join dk brown.
Row 55: Rep Row 7. Finish off dk brown; join off white.

Row 56: Purl.
Rows 57 through 60: Rep Rows 1 and 2 twice.
Row 61: Rep Row 7.

Row 62: Purl.
Rows 63 and 64: Rep Rows 1 and 2.
Row 65: Knit. Finish off, off white; join dk brown.

Row 66: Purl. Finish off dk brown; join off white.
Row 67: Rep Row 1 (1, 7, 7).
Row 68: Purl.

Rows 69 through 76: Rep Rows 1 and 2 four times. At end of Row 74, finish off, off white; join dk brown.

Row 77: Knit. Finish off dk brown; join off white.
Row 78: Purl.

Rows 79 through 84 (84, 90, 90): Rep Rows 1 and 2 three (three, six, six) times.

Note: Sleeve should measure about 17" (17", 18", 18").

Bind off.

Finishing
Step 1: Hold Front and Back with right sides together. Sew shoulder seams, leaving about 10" opening in center for neck.

Step 2: Sew sleeves to body between markers, matching center of sleeves to shoulder seams.

Weave in all loose ends.

Rows 9 and 10: Rep Rows 1 and 2. At end of Row 10, finish off, off white; join dk brown.

Row 11: Knit. Finish off dk brown; join off white.
Row 12: Purl.
Row 13: Rep Row 7.

Row 14: Purl.
Rows 15 through 18: Rep Rows 1 and 2 twice.
Row 19: Rep Row 7.

Row 20: Purl.
Row 21: Knit. Finish off, off white; join dk brown
Row 22: Purl. Finish off dk brown; join off white.

Rows 23 and 24: Rep Rows 1 and 2.
Row 25: Rep Row 7.
Row 26: Purl.

Rows 27 through 30: Rep Rows 1 and 2 twice.
Row 31: Rep Row 7.
Row 32: Purl. Finish off, off white; join dk brown.

Ripple Afghan

Ripple stitch patterns — achieved by working alternately spaced decreases and increases — are probably the most popular patterns for knitted afghans. This design combines an easy pattern with bright, contrasting colors. You should feel free to change the colors to match your own decor.

Using Circular Needles

Circular knitting needles are used for two reasons: first, to work a piece in the round with no seams, and second, to accommodate a large number of stitches that would be too crowded on a straight needle.

Circular needles come with points in the same sizes as straight needles, but with different lengths to the cable, which links the two points. The pattern will always tell you both the size and the length of the circular needle you will need.

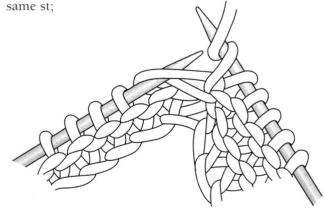

circular needle

For this pattern we use the circular needle to carry the large number of stitches — 279 — that are required. The work is not joined into a tube, but is worked flat just as if you were using straight needles.

To start, cast on in the usual manner.

> **Hint:** *When casting on a large number of stitches, it is helpful to place a marker on the needle after each 20 stitches, so that you don't have to keep counting and recounting the stitches.*

Now knit the first stitch of the first row into the last stitch that you cast on. Continue working across the row just as you would with straight needles. At the end of the row, switch the points to the opposite hands to begin a new row.

Size:
About 46" x 65" before fringe

Materials:
Worsted weight yarn, 14 oz (980 yds) off white; 10 1/2 oz (735 yds) rose; 14 oz (980 yds) dk rose; 7 oz (490 yds) each, aqua and dk aqua, or colors of your choice

Size 9, 36" length circular needles, or size required for gauge

Gauge:
9 sts = 2" in stock st

Pattern Stitch

Row 1: K1; sl 1 as to knit, K1, PSSO; * K9, double dec (to work double dec: insert right-hand needle into next 2 sts as if to knit; do not knit, but instead sl these 2 sts tog to right-hand needle; K1, pass both sl sts tog over knit st = double dec made); rep from * across row to last 12 sts; K9, K2 tog; K1.

Row 2: P6; * double inc (to work double inc: purl next st but leave st on left-hand needle; YO and purl again in same st;

now sl st off left-hand needle = double inc made); P9; rep from * across row to last 7 sts; double inc; P6. (**Note:** *on next row, work each YO as one st.*)

Rep Rows 1 and 2 for patt.

Ripple Afghan Instructions are on page 32.

Instructions

With dk rose, cast on 279 sts. Do not join; work back and forth in rows. Work in Pattern Stitch using the following 44-row color sequence. Cut yarn at end of each color sequence. Add new yarn at beg of next sequence.

6 rows dk rose

6 rows rose

10 rows off white

2 rows aqua

2 rows dk aqua

2 rows aqua

10 rows off white

6 rows rose

Rep 44-row color sequence 6 times more; then work 6 rows dk rose.

Bind off loosely in pattern as follows: K1, sl 1, K1, PSSO, bind off one st; * bind off next 9 sts; sl 2 as to knit, K1, pass both slipped sts over tog, bind off one st; rep from * across row to last 11 sts; bind off next 9 sts, K2 tog; bind off rem sts.

Weave in all loose ends.

Fringe

Cut a piece of cardboard 14 1/2" long and 6" wide. Wind dk rose loosely and evenly lengthwise around cardboard. When card is filled, cut yarn across one end. Do this several times, then make fringe as follows:

Hold 6 strands of yarn together, then fold in half. Hold afghan with right side facing you. Use crochet hook to draw folded end through stitch from right to wrong side (**A and B**);

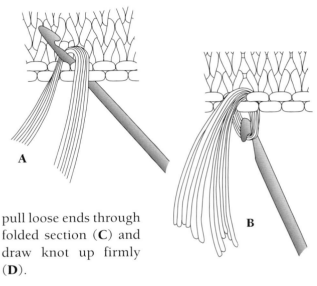

A

pull loose ends through folded section (**C**) and draw knot up firmly (**D**).

B

Tie knots in each point and in each valley across each short end of afghan. Trim ends evenly.

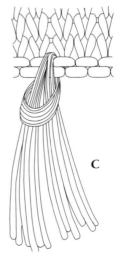

C

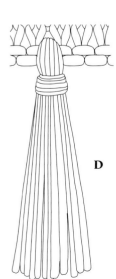

D